Frequently Asked Questions on Decentralisation in Uganda

Sylvester Wenkere Kisembo

MAKERERE UNIVERSITY
Kampala

FOUNTAIN PUBLISHERS
Kampala

Fountain Publishers Ltd
P.O. Box 488
Kampala, Uganda
E-mail:fountain@starcom.co.ug
Website:www.fountainpublishers.co.ug

Makerere University
P. O. Box 7062
Kampala, University

Distributed in Europe, North America and Australia by African Books
Collective Ltd (ABC), Unit 13, Kings Meadow, Ferry Hinksey Road,
Oxford OX2 0DP, United Kingdom.
Tel: 44(0) 1865-726686, Fax: 44(0)1865-793298.
E-mail: abc@africanbookscollective.com
Website: www.africanbookscollective.com

ISBN (10) 9970-02-609-7
ISBN (13) 978-9970-02-609-8

Dedication

Dedicated to the author's family and all the good practitioners and implementors of decentralisation in Uganda.

Contents

Foreword

Sylvester Wenkere Kisembo's place in scholarship and the implementation of the Decentralisation Programme as a governance alternative system in Uganda is distinguished. He was a god send, an insightful and practical intellectual who, from the commencement of the idea of decentralised governance in Uganda, was committed to nursing, nurturing and nourishing the idea until his untimely death in 2003. At the birth of the Innovations at Makerere Programme (I@Mak), he dedicated himself to educating Makerere on decentralisation. Kisembo thought and worked gallantly, but never superciliously.

Before his death, Kisembo had been commissioned by the I@Mak Committee to develop two sets of publications to educate the Makerere University community and to enable partnering institutions to comprehend and appreciate decentralisation. The goal was to sensitise the teaching staff, in particular, to review and revise old curricula or introduce a set of new courses to achieve the major objectives of decentralised service delivery in Uganda. Tragically, he died before completing his work. In spite of his battle with terminal cancer, Kisembo worked tirelessly on his assignment to the end and twice revised to the two texts – the Frequently Asked Questions (FAQs) and the Handbook on Decentralisation. Those of us who were honoured to work with this dedicated person were physically and intellectually challenged by Kisembo to continue his efforts on decentralisation.

The Publication Board, on behalf of I@Mak, decided to publish the two texts in honour of a man that had contributed so much to the cause of decentralisation. The texts have been only lightly edited, as he wished, to delete redundancies and typographical errors. Future editions shall incorporate comments/new approaches to decentralisation raised by academics, practitioners and policy makers.

The history of Kisembo in relation to decentralised governance in Uganda is like that of a mother and a child. He worked with the Decentralisation Secretariat, Ministry of Local Government, from its birth in 1992 until his death in 2003. He participated in the debate and drafting of the 1992 Resistance Council (RC) Statute, which formally enforced decentralised governance in Uganda. He later helped formulate the Local Government Act, 1997, and as chief of Finance Division of the Decentralisation Secretariat, he helped draft laws that formed the basis of the relevant guidelines and associated manuals to operationalising the Local Government Act. Notable among these were the Local Government Financial And Accounting Regulations (LGFAR) 1998, which forms the basis of the fiduciary management practices in the Local Governments Act.

We remember Kisembo as the unsung hero of the decentralisation policy in Uganda. He made several study tours to other countries in Africa to study their respective models of decentralisation. In collaboration with a number of his colleagues, he developed a home grown model of decentralisation based on complete devolution of powers, roles and responsibilities to local governments.

Kisembo was also elected a delegate to the Constituent Assembly in 1994 to debate the draft national constitution, which was finally enacted and promulgated as the supreme law in 1995. Thanks to his experience in decentralisation, the Ministry of Local Government regularly deployed him to resolve conflicts in local governments. Whenever the

Minister of Local Government toured local government areas, for example, he requested Kisembo to formulate answers to possible questions that might arise during the tour. When Makerere approached him to document the most frequently questions on decentralisation, Kisembo not only knew the terrain very well, he also had the right answers. We said BRAVO!

The Frequently Asked Questions are therefore based on the long practical experience of an intellectual, practitioner and founder member of decentralised governance in Uganda. They may not be exhaustive, and indeed they cannot be, since new challenges continue to emerge. However, together with the Handbook on Decentralisation, this text provides a wealth of information on decentralisation and a good number of feasible solutions to challenges facing new and old districts alike.

We are indebted to his family for their help and for having been there for him to the end while he was writing these two texts. We are sure that, had he lived to write the acknowledgement page, he himself would have thanked them, as well as many of his colleagues and associates at the Decentralisation Secretariat in the Ministry of Local Government. Most of all, we are grateful to Kisembo for his confidence and trust that we would bring his two texts to print. The texts are posthumous, but our heroic educator, practitioner and brilliant forebear is alive in print and memory.

May his soul rest in eternal peace.

Nakanyike B. Musisi and Samwiri Katuguka
Kampala 2005

Introduction

The Decentralisation Policy was announced by the President in October 1992, though prior to that date, steps had already been taken to legalise the systems. For example, in 1987, the National Resistance Council passed the Resistance Councils and Committees Statute, which introduced a completely new structure of local government.

The 1987 statute was followed by the Resistance Committees (Judicial Powers) Statute No 1 of 1988, and towards the end of 1993 the Local Government (Resistance Councils) Statute No 15.

The aim of these laws was to introduce a decentralisation system that would meet local needs.
Eventually, the constitution of 1995 consolidated the process and the Local Governments Act No. 1 of 1997 provided the legal framework in accordance with the new constitution. Changes in the local government system were quite fundamental, given that the country had been governed under a centralised system for a considerable period.

The minister responsible for local governments and many senior officials from the ministry toured the country to explain the implications of the new law and the new local government system as contained in the Act. During these tours, 190 questions relating to both the law and the new system that was to be introduced were asked.

The most frequently asked questions that cut across all the districts are reproduced in this handbook. The answers to the questions are based on the author's understanding of the local government system in Uganda, and his involvement in the decentralisation process.

The law and, in particular, the constitution and the Local Governments Act 1997 have been quoted where without recourse to a purely legalistic approach.

Section 1

Financial Management in General

Accountability

Q1. What is the role of the Local Governments Public Accounts Committee in combating corruption in the local government system?

A. The Local Governments Public Accounts Committee (LGPAC) as established under the Local Governments Act 1997 Sections 89 and 90 and also the Local Governments (Amendment Act 13) Sections 30 and 31 introduces a few changes in the principal Act.

The Act and the regulations issued under Statutory Instruments Supplement No 10 of 2000 govern the operations of the committees. The Act, for instance, defines the responsibilities of the committees as follows:

(i) To examine reports of the internal auditors and the Auditor-General.
(ii) To study the reports of the commissions of inquiry.
(iii) To submit its reports to the council and to the minister responsible for local governments.

The regulations of 2000 add the following accountability responsibilities:

Regulation 25 states that the committee should promote and foster strict accountability in the management of public affairs and use of resources and should support the responsibilities of the Inspector-General of Government, which include the elimination of corruption and abuse of office/authority of public office. The regulations also encourage the committees to supervise the enforcement of the leadership code, to ensure that the Inspector-General's functions of arrest, cause to arrest, prosecute or cause prosecution in respect of cases involving corruption and abuse of authority or public office are carried out.

Q2.   Who is an accounting officer of the funds from the centre to the urban councils?

A. Section 65 of the Local Governments Act 1997 appoints a Chief Administrative Officer of a district both as a head of the service of that district and as its accounting officer.

There are two levels of accountability regarding funds from the centre to the urban councils:

(i)   If funds have been locally generated and collected by an urban council, the Town Clerk of that council is in line with Section 66 (2) of the Act.

(ii)   Where the funds have been sent from the centre through the Chief Administrative Officer and accounting officer of the district, then he/she is accountable to both the urban council and the centre where funds were sent from.

Q3.   How are internal auditors protected against victimisation while performing their duties?

A. Internal auditors are public officers. Technically, therefore, they are protected by the rules, regulations and the law which establish the service and the District Service Commission in particular.

Standing Orders, for instance, provide a procedure for disciplining public officers. Stages are set clearly in these rules, starting with issuing a verbal a warning, written reprimand, interdiction or suspension and, finally, if the District Service Commission is satisfied that all the steps have been exhausted and there is no improvement in the behaviour of the officers, dismissal.

If however, an Internal Auditor is dismissed without following the rules and regulations, then that officer has to follow procedures to ensure that he/she is not victimised. Such an officer can appeal to the Public Service Commission under section 60 (2) of the Local Governments Act 1997. In some cases, the Inspector-General of Government has intervened. Courts of law have also been approached by a number of public officers who felt that they were being victimised.

Q4.   What should councils do if a local government body or official resists an audit?

A. The law provides for institutions that should be audited. Generally, any institution/organisation receiving public funds is subject to audit. The terms and conditions require finance officers to keep books of account and written financial statements for submission to responsible authorities. Requirements should clearly indicate when and how financial statements should be submitted and whether they would need auditing.

In many cases, the Auditor-General or internal auditor can audit public funds at any time (surprise audits). Individuals in local government should not keep council's money unless authorised by the council. Under the Local Governments Accounting and Financial Regulations, the accounting officer should give written authority for such officials to hold money.

These officers would include:
(i)   Cashiers
(ii) Revenue Collectors
(iii) Any other authorised officer. Should any officer fail to account for funds and refuses to be subjected to an audit, then the accounting officer (not the council) should alert CID (Criminal Investigation Department) to arrest or investigate the officer while the audit also takes place.

Institutions under local government control that could resist audit include schools and health units. In such cases, the headmaster of a school or the person in charge of the health centre could be arrested if he/she fails to account for the funds entrusted to him or her and resists being audited. The Local Governments Financial and Accounting Regulations state that an officer should hand over all the books of accounts and other required documents to auditors.

Q5.   How can councils sell off assets that are no longer required?

A. Technically such assets have no book value or have been written off by auditors (NIL BOOK VALUE). However, having a NIL book-value does not necessarily mean that the assets cannot fetch money on the open market. Such assets could be too expensive for the public institution to utilise but still useful and valuable to others.

In such a situation the council should resort to the Local Governments Financial and Accounting Regulations 1998. The regulations provide guidance and generally recommends transparency through public auction. Public auctions in the local government system is normally done by the Local Governments Tender Boards.

Q6. **How do you handle a case where an accounting officer misappropriates funds of a council?**

A. It must be established whether the accounting officer has misappropriated funds. This is normally determined by preliminary investigations carried out by the internal auditor or external auditor.

At this stage one of the two things could happen:

(i) Where the external auditor establishes that the accounting officer has actually misappropriated funds, the report is sent to the Local Governments Public Accounts Committee who should demand an explanation from the officer concerned. Since this is an external auditor's report with high probabilities of accuracy, the committee could also hand over the officer to the police.

(ii) However, should the report of misappropriation come from the internal auditor to the Local Governments Public Accounts Committee and other stakeholders, the LGPAC and the council could call on the expertise of the Auditor-General to verify the information, and then the next step is decided on after the verification. The idea is that all possible errors should be avoided in handling such cases.

Lack of accountability by the accounting officer does not necessarily mean that funds have been misappropriated. Lack of accountability usually means lack of proof that expenditure was incurred for official purposes. The accounting officer therefore needs time to produce evidence that public funds were properly used. When such evidence cannot be produced, and auditors have produced evidence e.g., funds did not go through the books of the local government accounting system or were withdrawn without following procedures as laid down in the regulations, the accountable person may be called to order.

Q7.   Is it in order for the council chairperson to scrutinise financial statements?

A. Though everybody has a right to scrutinise public financial statements since funds belong to the taxpayers and the chairperson actually represents taxpayers, such a course of action should be avoided as far as possible, to minimise conflict in administration.

(i)   The law does not give powers to the chairperson to involve himself/herself in financial matters. The accounting function is a responsibility of public officers, and particularly the accounting officers.

(ii) The role of the Executive Committee which the chairperson presides over has the responsibility of appointing various boards, including the Local Governments Public Accounts Committee, who should handle financial matters on behalf of the council. However, should a chairperson take an interest in a financial statement which he/she believes has a problem regarding accountability, it is advisable to be transparent and call upon the internal auditor, or even the external auditor, to assist to interpreting such statements. The chairperson should hand over the matter to other organs of the council, as soon as possible for example, the Local Governments Public Accounts Committee, the internal auditors or even external auditors.

Q8. **Who has the overall responsibility for funds of the division?**

A. The following must be clarified first in order to answer the question and, secondly, to elaborate on the law and regulations:

(i) A division by law is a local government and as such it is accountable to its electorate for funds.

(ii) A division is either a city division council or a municipal division.

In such a case, therefore, the Town Clerk of the City or Municipal Council would be the overall accounting officer of all the divisions in the city or division. An Assistant Town Clerk of a division is accountable to the Town Clerk of the city or municipal council. Furthermore a City or Municipal Town Clerk is charged with the responsibility accountability of the area under his/her jurisdiction.

Q9.   How long does it take for the Auditor-General to release audit reports after the audit exercise?

A. Section 87 of the Act specifies that books of account should be given to the Auditor-General for audit four months after the close of the Financial Year.

The law does not specify when the Auditor-General should present his/her report to authorities and bodies as outlined in the Act. However, the tradition is that, six months after books have been presented, the Auditor-General issues his/her report.

Q10.   How can collusion between the sub-accountant and chairperson of a sub-county to misappropriate council funds be avoided?

A. If top officials of any organisation collude to defraud the institution they are supposed to protect, then there is very little that can be done. However, a system is in place or should be in place to ensure that checks and balances exist to protect the public.

(i) Section 91 of the Act provides for an internal auditor for the local governments system, who is supposed to be strong enough to ensure that public funds are not misappropriated in a fraudulent manner.

(ii) The Auditor-General has decentralised the services of the department. Every district must have an Auditor-General's district office. The law allows the Auditor-General to carry out surprise audits and checks. Normally, signals of theft would be easily "noticed", for example contractors may not be paid or the revenue to be remitted to the district may not come as regularly as in other sub-counties.

(iii) There are other state organs that should take an interest in what is happening in a sub-county. For example, the Internal Security Organisation (ISO) makes reports to the RDC on what is happening in individual sub-counties.

Q11. **What is the relationship between the Town Clerk of a municipality and the Assistant Town Clerk in a division? Does this Relationship allow the Town Clerk at the municipal level to sign financial instruments of a division?**

A. A municipal Town Clerk has the overall responsibility for financial management, as the accounting officer of the whole municipality. There are bank accounts and other transactions that may not be effectively operated unless he/she signs, for example, a collection account funds are distributed to other local governments and administrative units. The relationship between the two is that of supervisor and a junior. A municipal Town Clerk supervises the Assistant Town Clerk in charge of a division.

Q12. **What is your advice on failure of districts to remit 65% of its collections to the sub-counties?**

A. The main challenge is the capacity of sub-counties to establish how much the District owes in terms of revenue collected at the district level. Once such amounts are established, the law allows a local government to withhold remittance equal to what it is owed.

It is also important to establish which revenue a district collects on behalf of the sub-counties. Where transparency exists, a district should make a return or returns to all sub-counties indicating the amounts each sub-county is entitled to. Such transparency should help minimise conflicts between the two levels.

Q13. **The CAOs are the only officers who know how much money is remitted to districts. They sometimes use their positions to misappropriate these funds. How can the RDCs and district chairpersons know what is remitted to the districts, and to guard against misappropriation?**

A. The process of remitting funds to districts should be as transparent as possible. The CAO is expected to account for the following funds to the district:

(i)   Local Revenue from sub-counties and other contracted outsources. This source is known by all councillors and the Executive Committee. The internal auditor should be able to trace any fraud.

(ii) Funds from the central government are normally published in newspapers. The public and other stakeholders should follow up these remittances.

(iii) Funds from donors, particularly NGOs, whose funds do not go through the Treasury, may not be known by the public. However, the Executive

Committee would know, and that is one of the many reasons why they are empowered to monitor and co-ordinate activities of NGOs in a district.

Q14. How do you handle a case of an accounting officer who misappropriates the funds of a council?

A. Internal procedures exist that would prevent one person to misappropriate funds of the council. There is the Chief Internal Auditor, heads of department or directorates who are supposed to utilise those funds and the Budget Committee, which reviews the work plans and makes adjustments in allocations, etc.

The RDC is also entitled to inquire and to be given information on the inflows (and outflows) of funds should it be considered necessary. However, it the accounting officer misappropriates funds, he/she should be handed over to the CID and other organs that handle such situations.

Q15. How can corruption be eliminated, when the IGG's office is not adequately backed by local council activities?

A. The Inspector General of Government is established by the constitution and a special law (Act of Parliament). These legal instruments give the IGG considerable powers of investigations, etc. Should local government officials become unco-operative during investigations, the IGG can evoke sections of the Act which would force the officers to respond.

If activities are unethical, there is the Minister for Integrity and Ethics in the President's office can assist local government to ensure compliance with normal governments procedures. The IGG and the Directorate of Ethics and Integrity are expected to work together to eliminate corruption.

Q16.   Who authorises the withdrawals of funds from the bank at the sub-county level?

A. The banking procedures are well outlined in the Local Governments Financial and Accounting Regulations (LGFAR Part X VII Regulations 177-194).

A sub-county chief is an accounting officer of the area under his/her jurisdiction, in accordance with section 70 (2) of the Act. As an accounting officer, the sub-county chief can withdraw funds from the council's accounts. A sub-accountant can do the same, but the sub-county chief has to approve payments before they are made.

Q17.   Can a district reject a CAO if it isproved that he/she was involved in financial fraud?

A. A CAO is not posted from the centre. He/she is normally appointed by the District Service Commission. The DSC should select a person whose integrity is not questionable.

However, should it happen after appointment that the incumbent's integrity is now questionable, then the normal procedures should be followed:

(i) Proper investigations should be carried out by competent people or organs.

(ii) Information gathered against the officer should be handed over to competent organs of state for example, the IGG the District Service Commission, and the chairperson.

(iii) CID could also be involved.

If there is evidence of fraud, the Executive Committee should make a case to the District Service Commission. The officer should be asked to defend himself or herself. A balanced decision should be taken after evaluating all the available and well-researched information. In the case of fraud, the matter would be handled by CID. In case of other complaints, then the DSC can handle such matters.

Q18. **Can a public servant be a member of District Public Accounts Committee?**

A. There are two sources of guidance on this question:

(i) Local Government Act section 89, which establishes the committee as amended by Act No. 13 of 2001 section 30. The Act states that a member shall not be a member of a Local Government Administration or a Local Government Council. This does not seem to be a "blanket" ban on public servants in general. If, therefore, a central government official is allowed under the standing orders and other laws and regulations, he/she could be a member of the LGPAC.

(ii) The appointing authority can exclude a public officer if it so wishes. Technically, the appointing authority has powers to appoint anybody within the law. It could also avoid appointment of public servants without giving any reason.

Q19.   How can the finances of a sub-county which has no finance committee be supervised?

A. The law does not prohibit a finance committee as such. It provides for standing committees and one of them could be charged with the responsibility of finances. It seems there are no special duties for a finance committee as such. Other organs seem to exist to handle special duties of finance committees as they used to exist in the past, for example, the tendering function is now carried out by a special board. Queries, etc are handled by the Local Governments Public Accounts Committee and also the Executive Committee. These bodies seem to reduce the relevancy of a specialised finance committee as they carry out supervisory roles.

Q20.   Is it in order for a person who audits the sub-county books of account to write and give a copy of his/her findings to the sub-county council?

A. The devolution of powers and functions mean that accountability has been devolved to the local government level, in this case to LC III (sub-county). Whether it is internal or external auditor, he/she has an obligation to give a report of audited accounts to the council concerned. The council can accept challenges or even reject the audited reports. The auditor is expected to defend his/her findings.

Normally, auditors' reports are divided into two phases. The first phase is given to the council and the accounting officer responds to some of issues, normally called queries, raised in the report. The auditor could decide to give the draft to both the accounting officer and the Executive Committee (not the full council).

Once the queries have been responded to, then the final report is issued. It is difficult for the accounting officer to challenge the findings of the auditor at this stage.

It is, however, unlikely for the Executive Committee to submit a draft report to the full council. They normally submit the final report to the council at which point the Public Accounts Committee intervenes to implement the recommendations of the report. The auditors do not have powers to implement their own report.

Q21. **Is it acceptable for a district to have a pseudo-clearing house before finance questions can be resolved?**

A. Clearing houses are unnecessary. These existed under the old law (section 18 of 1967 Act) where the centre was in charge of local administration and there was lack of transparency in the system.

The current law provides for the following:
(i)   Executive Committee, which supervises other organs, of a council.
(ii) Standing Committees, which actually "supervise" the Executive Committee and reports to the council.

(iii) Public Accounts Committee (LGPAC) which implements the auditor's report and takes action against those reported to have gone against the financial and accounting regulations and other regulations issued, including conditions accompanying conditional grants.

(iv) The Local Governments Tender Boards – which carry out procurements.

This institutional framework therefore has no room for a "clearing house". To the above list of institutions and organs can be added the internal audit section, which carries out supervisory activities of the accounting function. The Internal Audit Section is independent of Chief Finance Officer and the accounting officer.

Q22.   What is the implication of a district re-allocating donor funds?

A. It is necessary to define the word "donor". There are many donors assisting local governments and not all of them have similar conditionalities.

(i)   In the case of international donors, for example the World Bank, DANIDA, DFID, etc, most of the funds go through the central government under the sector-wide-approah (SWAP). Such funds target PEAP (Poverty Eradication Action Plan) and the central government is bound by agreements between the donors and itself to spend the money only to those agreed–upon programme(s).

(ii) Some donors also contribute towards specific needs of some districts. For example, DANIDA has been supporting Rakai under the district wide-approach (DWA) where a plan of the whole district is drawn by the district itself and DANIDA finances areas of interest. Donors can accept re-allocation within the overall support programme as long as the council provides convincing reasons. Other donors, like SNV and Irish AID, Austrian Aid, etc. operate in different districts, where re-allocation can be negotiated.

Q23.   **What happens to a chairperson of a sub-county council who formulates a budget in his/her favour (emoluments) at the expense of the council?**

A.   The interpretation or clarification of the question is necessary. It seems to mean that the chairperson manipulates the budget process to increase the personal allowances of his office and other members of the Executive Committee contrary to what is provided for under the first schedule of the Act (and Statutory Instrument 2001 No. 38). In such a situation the council should reject the budget until the Executive Committee complies with the law which provides the amount each member of the executive committee is supposed to be paid.

A chairperson who operates without an approved budget should be reported to the ministry responsible for local governments, the IGG, or apply to court for an injunction.

Q24.   **How can the independence and funding of the Local Governments Public Accounts Committees be guaranteed when local government councils have the responsibility of vetting their funding?**

A. This question may not arise now. It used to arise before the funding of Local Governments Public Accounts Committees were funded by the central government from the Consolidated Fund (section 30 (d) Act 13 of 2001). The law was amended as indicated above in order to reduce temptations for district councils to compromise the independence of these committees. If councils still withhold parts of the funds in order that the members of LGPAC can be compromised, then that is wrong and can be reported to authorities at the centre.

Q25.   **How should the IGG and the auditors reports be handled by a district council?**

A. A district council's job has been made easier by the establishment of the Local Governments Public Accounts Committees, which receive reports and act against those who have violated the financial and accounting regulations.

Councils should encourage the committees to perform their duties, for example, through allowances and other incentives.

The law empowers the IGG's office to arrest and prosecute suspects and council should support the

IGG's efforts to curb wrongdoing. Council generally has no option but to take action against officers when LGPAC find them incompetent.

Q26. **What happens if a council passes a budget in a given fiscal year, but does not spend on the items budgeted amount even if the money is available?**

A. Local governments operate differently from the central system. If funds are not utilised in a given financial year, it is possible to carry forward the amount to the next financial year. However, this position could change with the new fiscal management system being introduced by the centre. Currently the centre does not carry forward balances at the end of the financial year. If the money is not carried to the F/Y, then it is returned to the general fund A/C.

Q27. **How can a council retrieve its money if one of its employees sells off its property?**

A. Selling council property without authority from a competent organ of the council is a criminal offence. The likely procedure would be to hand over the matter to police to make criminal charges against the person concerned. The next stage would be a civil case to recover the property. A competent legal department would be able to give appropriate advice.

Q28.   If a Town Clerk or a sub-county chief fails to produce a monthly financial report, what steps can be taken to avoid fraud?

A. Failure to submit one monthly report should not raise an alarm unless there is a strong suspicion that it was deliberate. Officials might fail to produce a report because of several reasons, which could be genuine. However, even if a monthly report is lacking, sample auditing can be done to establish the position of the council. For example, it can be established whether banking has taken place. It can also be established whether all payments were made against vouchers and if the cashbook was written. If not balanced such a task could be done in the shortest possible time to rule out any possible payments that were not entered into the cashbook, and cannot be traced.

Q29.   Can any councillor undertake to monitor utilisation of sub-county funds as an individual?

A. The law does not provide for such specific situations. However, a councillor representing a sub-county is entitled to monitor the implementation of the budget in his/her sub-county for a specific financial year. However, the councillor may not replace internal auditors or produce financial statements with regard to the utilisation of funds; since he may not have the knowledge and accurate records, let alone the authority to do so.

A councillor should comment on the quality of work (personal observations), the time being spent on specific jobs and whether or not objectives of the council are likely to be met.

Q30. **If a sub-county chief causes a financial loss to a third party, who should pay?**

A. If a sub-county chief causes a third party to experience financial loss during the performance of his/her duties, then the council has to meet the loss, make it good and pay back to the third party.

In such a case, the organs of the council would review the case and decide how to deal with the chief. Losses can be caused through negligence, ignorance, deliberate action or circumstances beyond the ability of the officer.

Q31. **If a councillor is responsible for the economic development of his/her area, why must he/she be barred from being a signatory on sub-county financial instruments/cheques?**

A. The law draws a line between political, financial and administrative accountability. A political leader (a councillor) has political accountability and he/she is involved in the policy making process, which is passed to administrators to implement and finance. A political leader has powers to check the implementation process of a system where responsibilities are shared. He/she introduces checks and balances necessary for the management of the country. If a councillor was involved in signing checks, etc, he/she would not be in a position to question administrators on issues relating to financial matters.

Q32.   Who is a signatory in the town council?

A. The financial and accounting procedures in local governments are provided for under the Local Governments Financial and Accounting Regulations 1998, which gives a tentative list of who should sign cheques and other financial instruments, final accounts and other financial statements.

There are two senior officers in the town council, namely, the Town Clerk, who as the accounting officer, is a principal signatory and the Chief Finance Officer, who should be the other signatory. These officers are appointed by the Executive Committee. Although the law does not mention them, it would be inappropriate for the Executive Committee to appoint junior staff and leave out the accounting officer.

The law gives the Executive Committee powers to appoint signatories, for example, when the administration and political leadership disagree.

Section 2

Centre – Local Fiscal Relationship

Q1. **How are grants from the centre to local governments determined?**

A. The constitution and the Act empowers the Local Government Finance Commission to determine grants to local governments. The base for the formula is found in the schedule of the constitution. However, considerable improvement has been made on that original formula. Improvements have introduced a number of parameters, such as population and area. Detailed calculations for grants to divisions, for instance, have other parameters, like school going age population, mortality rates etc.

Other special conditional grants, for example PMA non-sectoral grants, are based on a formula agreed upon between the commission and the line ministry concerned.

Q2. **Where do town councils draw funding for their roads network and when would this network be absorbed in the Feeder Road Scheme?**

A. Priority has been given to feeder road mainly because these roads provide critical linkages between rural and urban areas . The roads also link people to services, like schools and health facilities.

Town councils receive block or unconditional grants which they could use for urban roads if they so wish. There is no timetable as to when urban roads willbe funded in the same way the rural roads are being funded. Most likely the decision will be influenced by the importance of such roads.

Q3.   Why are donor funds not decentralised?

A. (i) Donor funds, including those for the sector-wide-approach, are actually decentralised to the extent that donors and the Uganda government agree to do so. The national budget is composed of over 50% donor funding. Programmes like PEAP are funded by donors and funds are allocated to local governments as conditional grants.

(ii) The second category of donor funds is that of donors who invest directly in local governments through various programmes, e.g. DANIDA in Rakai or SNV (Netherlands) in the West Nile region. These programmes are a result of negotiations between donors, the Uganda government and the local governments concerned. Programmes may not cover the whole country, but they are "decentralised" to the districts that benefit from such programmes.

Q4.   How are the salaries of civil servants determined?

A. There is a ministry responsible for the public service. The Ministry of Public service is entrusted with the responsibility of determining the terms of service of public officers, including salaries.

Salaries are determined on the basis of a number of factors, for example the ability of governments to collect taxes, the size of the public service and the macro-economic policies the government has adopted. The main focus of macro-economic policies is the control of inflation, the government's policy on the service delivery and the wage bill.

Q5. **How soon will government implement the policy of equalisation grants to boost the low revenue of poor districts?**

A. Equalisation grants have now been implemented. A formula is in place and many districts have benefited. The formula is subjèct to review from time to time, in order to determine who really deserves the equalisation grant.

Q6. **Why can't the centre grant local governments powers to contract, supervise and control funds on contract jobs, for example maintenance of major roads (trunk roads)?**

A. Trunk roads are not decentralised, partly because local governments do not have the capacity to sustain or supervise them. Secondly, these roads inter-link districts with different jurisdictions. Delegating similar responsibilities to several districts would cause problems. Thirdly, local governments have been too slow to utilise funds simply because local governments have not been able to enter into contracts, and as a result such funds have returned to the central government.

Q7.   Can town councils with peculiar problems be considered for greater Equalisation Grants?

A.   Local Governments have two bodies that represent their interests on the Local Governments Finance Commission, namely the Uganda Local Authorities Association (ULAA) and the Urban Authorities Association of Uganda (UAAU). The job of these representatives is to negotiate, advocate and put across the views and needs of their members. It is therefore possible to address special district needs over and above the equalisation grants.

Q8.   Can a division or sub-county obtain grants directly from the central government?

A.   These lower local governments receive grants from government directly for example under LGDP. However, a district or a city council is used as an agent of central government to ensure that funds reach their destination. There are about 1000 sub-counties, including town councils. It would be difficult and expensive for the central government to deal with each of them directly in all the transactions.

Q9.   Should districts stop funding delegated staff, for example prisons, police and works, for their salaries and services provided?

A.   Local governments do not have legal obligations to pay anybody outside their staff list. It is the responsibility of central government to pay its own employees. However, the central government can request local governments to pay by agreement and subject to a refund.

Sometimes, local governments obtain funds from the centre to meet wage and salary costs, acting as agents of the centre, in which case local governments are entitled to demand payment for the extra work carried out by their staff.

Q10. **If a district hosts a minister or central government officer, who should finance such activity?**

A. A district local government is a body corporate. It operates a budget and it has powers to spend on activities approved by the council. It has, therefore, powers to host a central government minister or any other public official.

If, however, it is a central government function, for example celebrations of independence, and the central government delegates such responsibilities, then it has the responsibility to settle the bills for functions required to finance such activities.

Q11. **From whom should women councils obtain funds to mobilise for votes?**

A. Women councils are outside the responsibility of local governments. It is up to those who organise women council elections to advise on how such activities should be financed.

Section 3

Councils and Councillors

Q1. **What is the procedure for the removal of a sub-county or town council chairperson? Who takes charge of the council after the chairperson has been removed?**

A. The removal of a sub-county or LC III chairperson is provided for under section 15 of the Act as amended by the Local Government (Amendment) Act No 13 of 2001. A notice in writing, must be given to the speaker of the district council, stating that the members intend to pass a resolution to remove the chairperson. The notice should be signed by not less than one third of the total members of the council. The chairperson can be removed from office for the following reasons:

(1) Abuse of office
(2) Corruption
(3) Incompetence
(4) Misconduct or misbehaviour
(5) Physical or mental incapacities
(6) Refusal to implement council decisions

Such a notice must clearly state the intentions of the council and the charges against the chairperson to be censured. Documented evidence should be provided together with the notice. A copy of the notice should be given to the chairperson and the Minister of Local Government.

The minister is required to constitute a tribunal within fourteen days, headed by a chief magistrate. After receiving a report of the tribunal, the speaker must convene a council meeting. In case of physical or mental incapacity, a report will be issued by a medical board, which establishes the medical status of the chairperson.

Where a tribunal establishes that the allegation against the chairperson contains substance of truth, then the council is convened and the report is presented to the council. The vote of no confidence in the chairperson requires a two-thirds majority.

Similar procedures are followed in the case of mental and physical incapacitation. If the medical board finds that the chairperson cannot perform his/her duties as expected because of his/her health status, the council is required to pass a resolution supported by two thirds of all members in order for the chairperson to be dismissed. In both cases, the chairperson is free to defend himself or herself and to be represented by a lawyer where necessary.

In the absence of a chairperson, and if a council has a speaker, the speaker assumes the responsibilities of the chairperson if the chairperson is not available or has been dismissed, or resigns. The speaker has no powers during the period of acting to reshuffle the Executive, to increase the number or to replace any vacant position of secretaries.

Q2. In cases where the local government council chairperson and vice chairperson are unable to perform their duties, who takes over from them?

A. The law provides that, if a chairperson is unable to carry out his/her duties, the speaker takes over the responsibilities, until another chairperson has been elected. The deputy speaker meanwhile takes over as speaker of the council.

Q3. What is the role of a district council in vetting the appointments of the members on a statutory body?

A. A council is responsible for the appointment of members of a statutory body. The executive committee proposes names. The council can reject either all of them or some of them, or confirm (approve) all those presented. However, the council ensures that the:

(i) Proposed members fulfil the required qualifications under the law.

(ii) Executive's proposal has taken into consideration the local political interests of various stakeholders. These could involve religious and tribal interests, where, for example, a district is made up of many tribes.

(iii) Council, through the vetting exercise, can eliminate possible corrupt practices.

(iv) Disadvantaged are represented.

Q4. **Can a public servant be a chairperson of a movement committee without resigning from the public service?**

A. It would be unacceptable for a public officer to play such political role while still employed by the Public Service Commission or District Service Commission. It is possible that he/she would be compromised while carrying out his/her duties as a civil servant. Standing orders prohibit such involvement in politics by public officers.

Q5. **Who should be the legal representative of the district, urban and sub-county councils?**

A. There are two levels of responsibilities:

(i) Political responsibility. At the political level, a chairperson or mayor takes responsibility of the area under his/her jurisdiction, as the political head of the area.

(ii) Administrative representation. The Chief Administrative Officer, the Town Clerk or sub-county chief have administrative powers and they are accounting officers in their areas of jurisdiction. They represent their councils where necessary.

Q6. **Can the property of a local government be attached by courts of law?**

A. Such attachment was possible before the amendment of the Local Government Act of 1997. The amended law does not allow attachment of councils' properties.

Q7. **What is the relationship between the secretary for security and the local defence unit, local police and other security forces?**

A. The secretary for security must be involved in policy issues affecting security in the area under his/her jurisdiction. The secretary for security should co-ordinate those forces that is under his/her control, for example, local police. However, he/she is not empowered to interfere with security bodies that were not decentralised.

Local defence units may be delegated to the district authorities, in which case they would fall under the secretary for defence. In most cases, the police work independently of district officials, but co-operate and co-ordinate operations where necessary.

Section 4

Financial Management

Q1. **Why do districts fail to submit 65% of the conditional grants to the sub-counties?**

A. The Local Governments Act Second Schedule carefully allocates or assigns responsibilities to each level of local government. A district is the highest level of local government. Accordingly, it has more responsibilities than lower level local governments. This means that it receives more funds to meet its obligations.

However, lately there are some specific grants that can be accessed by sub-county councils, for example, the NAADS grants and the PMA grants. Also under the LGDP (Local Governments Development Programme) there are other grants which go directly (through the district) to the LC III.

Q2. **How do urban councils relate to district councils on matters of finance?**

A. Under both the constitution and the Act, urban councils are financially independent of districts on financial matters, though they are lower local government councils.

Some linkages can be established administratively, particularly in the collection of revenue. Urban councils, below city councils, also share the Local Governments Public Accounts Committee.

A town council which chooses not to have a tender board, a district and a town council can opt to share a Local Government Tender Board.

Q3.   What is the role of councillors regarding the management of finances of their local councils?

A. There are many indirect and to some extent direct possible interventions for councillors in the financial management of councils' funds.

    (i)   Budgeting – councillors play a useful role in the budgeting processes of councils. Budgets are defined as financial plans for councils.

    (ii) Implementation of budgets i.e. work plans are subject to approval by councillors. This also involves the allocation or re-allocation of financial resources.

    (iii) Councillors play a useful role in revenue mobilisation.

    (iv) Executive Committees are empowered to, at the end of each year, review the performance of their council against the work plans set out during the financial year (F/Y) (value for money).

Q4.   Is it acceptable to spend funds when the council has not approved the budget?

A. One of the powers entrusted to local governments by the constitution and the Act is the approval of budgets before money is expended. Section 82 of the

Act defines the financial year as stretching from 1 July current year to 30 June of the following year. Section 83, on the other hand, specifically bans a council from utilising public funds without approval by councillors in a council meeting. The law provides that the budget be presented by 15 June, so that a council can approve a Vote-On-Account (VOA) by 1 July. A VOA is necessary in order to give a council reasonable time to debate allocations in the estimates.

Q5.   How are the funds remitted to the parish and village councils utilised?

A. Sections 82 and 83 quoted above actually apply to all councils from the district to the village council. These councils are supposed to budget, approve their estimates and work plans and spend money accordingly. However, in practice, this may not happen in every parish and village council. There are many reasons why, but most important is lack of capacity to budget and supervise the implementation of those budgets.

Q6.   What are the functions of the Finance Committee at sub-county level?

A. A Finance Committee as such does not exist in the legal framework of the local government system. The law provides for executive committees at the sub-county level to handle most of the issues that would ordinarily be vested in standing committees at the district level.

Q7.   **In determining the 15% to be utilised by the councils, committees and boards, do you base the percentage on the amount before or after remitting 35% to the District Council?**

A.   The 15% is based on the amount available and at the disposal of the council to use and implement its plans. The 15% should be part of the budget of the sub-county or any other council, which is required by law to meet those expenses. The law also requires that it should be based on the actual income, not merely estimates.

Q8.   **How are the funds allocated to departments in a local government i.e. at district, sub-county, municipal, town and division levels?**

A.   The allocation to various departments and directorates is determined by a number of factors:

(i)   Some departments implement central government programmes. In such cases they access funds "ear-marked" for specific purpose directly from the centre.

(ii)   However, under normal local governments allocations, negotiations should start in standing committees and in the executive committee where each secretary should put a case for the budget he/she is supposed to supervise. Standing and executive committees should agree on allocation of funds before the debate in council.

Q9. **Who is responsible for presenting the council budget?**

A. The law does not specify who should present a local government budget in the council. However, there are two options available.

(i) The chairperson can decide to present the budget as the political head of the area under his/her jurisdiction.

(ii) He /she can, on the other hand, ask one of the secretaries (member of the Executive Committee) to do so, particularly the secretary in charge of finances. The speaker should not present a budget.

Q10. **Given the low tax base in some districts, does the law allow for village and parish councils to operate joint accounts and utilise the funds on joint projects?**

A. The first schedule of the Act gives powers to council to carry out joint projects. Such projects can be carried out in many ways without the need for a joint account, depending on how the councils decide. consolidating financial resources can be done with or without joint accounts.

Q11. **Clarify the provisions of the law regarding the 35% remittance from the municipal/city council to the divisions?**

A. This provision involves two important decentralisation principles:

(i) Non-subordination i.e. a division is not a subordinate of the city or municipal council but a local government in its own right, with obligations that should be met from entitled financial and other resources.

(ii) Financial autonomy.

Based on the these two principles, the fifth schedule of the Act Regulation 14 requires a city or municipal council to remit to the city or municipal division 30% of the total revenue collected as grants. These grants must be based on a formula as provided.

The formula basically addresses imbalances in the development of individual divisions. It takes into consideration the number of primary school age children This was quite appropriate at the time before implementation of UPE. The principle still holds, since UPE has not achieved 100% attendance.

It also addresses equity in health, by considering child mortality, number of residents, etc. The 30%, therefore, is put aside each year and, using the above formula, distributed to the divisions. In the end, the disadvantaged divisions, according to the formula, receive most of the funds.

In practice, however, the city/municipal councils have resisted paying this grant because they claim that the distribution of responsibilities between the divisions and the higher councils is not balanced. City and municipal councils argue that they have more responsibilities than the remittances they receive from both the centre as grants and the 35% of local revenue from the divisions.

Q12.   **Why does the Minister of Local Government send teams to the local governments to write books of account?**

A.   Since decentralisation is a new policy, local governments have not yet developed capacity to satisfy central government legal and accountability requirements. Secondly, writing the books of account is the best way to monitor local governments' compliance with accountability, rules, regulations and procedures. Finally, the law requires, in sections 96 to 99 of the Act, that line ministries should provide technical assistance, co-ordinate, mentor and advocate local governments, particularly the ministry responsible for local governments.

Q13.   **What are the procedures established for the management of revenue accruing from the activities of land boards?**

A.   District land boards are supposed to be self-accounting bodies. At the same time, they must be included in the budgets of district councils.

Revenue from land is presumably handled under the land boards regulations and also under the LGFAR, since the Boards are under the councils' jurisdiction. Therefore (the councils) can:

(i)   Allow the boards to collect land revenue as a non-tax revenue or Appropriation-in-Aid (AID) and add on extra revenue if the amount collected is not sufficient for the Boards' activities.   If the Land Board collects more revenue than the approved budget, the surplus should be passed on to the district treasury as district revenue.

(ii) The district council could, on the other hand, demand all the revenue collected from the Boards' activities and incorporate all such revenue into one Revenue account (The General Revenue A/ C) and Budget for the Board's Activities from the Consolidated Income of the district.

Q14. Why should the county council receive 5% of the revenue generated by a sub-county when it is only an administrative unit and not a local government?

A. Administrative units, like the county council, do not have as much power as local government councils. Accordingly, the second schedule does not mention their functions. However, section 49 of the main Act defines their responsibilities, which, inter-alia, include:

(i) Resolving problems or disputes referred to it by the relevant sub-county or village councils.

(ii) Monitoring the delivery of services within its area of jurisdiction.

(iii) Assisting in the maintenance of law and order and security.

(iv) Carrying out any other assignment from the district council or higher local government councils. (A municipal council can be considered a higher local government council.) The functions imposed by the law as outlined above require funds and, therefore, the 5% is justified.

Q15. **What is advised regarding administrative units which have little financial resources but enormous development projects?**

A. In law, administrative units should not have too many development projects in addition to those provided under section 49. However, a higher local government e.g. a district, can assign responsibilities to an administrative unit. In such a case the local government assigning such responsibilities should provide funds. This is a fundamental principle in a decentralised setting. If such funds are not made available, the administrative council should decline to carry out the responsibilities.

Q16. **Why do current local councillors earn less than previous councillors?**

A. Generally, the law does not state exactly how much a councillor should earn. However, the law sets the percentage of actual revenue collected by a council during the previous F/Y. Councillors' allowances therefore depend on how much their councils collect from local revenue sources.

Most likely the previous councillors' referred to in the question were those elected under statute 15 of 1993 Local Government (Resistance Councils) Statute. There was no formula according to which councillors were paid. However, councils do not pay uniform amounts. Some councils may pay more now than under the replaced statute, depending on the success of revenue collection.

Q17.   Can a sub-county borrow funds from a bank?

A. A sub-county council, as a local government, can borrow under regulation 20 of the Fifth Schedule of the Act. However, such loans can only be authorised by the minister responsible for local governments. The conditions and requirements are stiff, intended to ensure that funds are borrowed for serious business and the council itself considers the need as a priority. Other conditions include the need for the Auditor General to provide an unqualified Annual Audit Report.

Q18.   How often should the Finance Committee sit to apportion unconditional grants received by a district?

A. As already explained elsewhere in this handbook, there is no such thing as a Finance Committee, but there could be a standing committee which handles finance, among other functions.

However, such a committee need not handle the unconditional grant every time it is received. A council should have an approved budget if the unconditional grant is part of its own revenue and allocated right from the start of each financial year. The Executive Committee and standing committees can review work plans from time, to time according to funds available. Through reallocations, unconditional grants would be affected.

Q19. **Can a district council budget for the sitting allowances of members of statutory boards?**

A. Though funds for most of the statutory boards come from the consolidated fund (centre), district councils have responsibilities to budget for them. All funds to be utilised by a district council should appear in their budget regardless of the source.

Q20. **What should be done if interested groups like the youth, women and persons with disabilities are not catered for in the budget?**

A. Where such groups were left out of the budget, the budget desk must:

(i) Identify funds for reallocation .

(ii) Prepare supplementary estimates to cater for the omitted groups. Reallocation must take place within the existing approved estimates.

Q21. **Can the ACAO veto the financial matters of a sub-county without breaching the Local Governments Financial and Accounting Regulations?**

A. The Assistant Chief Administrative Officer (ACAO) has no powers to veto the decisions of a local government council. Should his/her advice be ignored, auditors should be called in to make a recommendation to the accounting officer (CAO). The CAO should then act accordingly. It should be in the interest of the sub-county to stop any further financial transactions until the minister's advice is sought, if necessary.

Q22.   How long after a budget was tabled, should it be passed?

A. In theory, a budget could take a few months, for example three to four months when a VOT is being used, before it is formally approved. However, so time much is not necessary. Most of the budget process would have been completed long before the presentation of the budget to the council. It is possible therefore for council to approve its budget within a few weeks. This saves money on sitting allowances. Besides, district councils, for instance, have a limited number of times they are obliged to meet per year, because of financial constraints.

Q23.   Should a division share part of the unconditional grants extended to a municipal council?

A. There is no law to stop such revenue sharing. However, municipal councils normally argue that such grants are not even sufficient for their own needs. In such cases, divisions may appeal to the local governments finance commission for intervention, if they feel strongly that they need unconditional grants.

Q24.   If a sub-county cannot generate enough revenue for its programme, how can they obtain money for development, as the 65% retention would not suffice?

A. Decentralisation is a challenge to the local government system. The purpose of assigning sources of revenue to local governments was to ensure that they (local governments) meet their obligations, both in terms of revenue collection and implementation of programmes.

However, currently many special grants go directly to sub-counties, for various programmes like NAADS and PMA. Also, under the LGDP, sub-counties can receive grants, which can be spent on programmes that are identified by the councils, provided they fall within national priorities.

Q25. **How can local authorities' creditors obtain their money without resorting to costly legal battles?**

A. Prudent financial management principles are the key to financial problems of most local governments. Once local governments fail to manage their cash flows effectively, they are likely to cause financial loss to creditors. Suppliers, should therefore, should judge the capacity of a local government to pay before supplies are made on credit. It would be in their own interests to refuse to supply a poorly managed local government.

Q26. **Can an individual borrow from a local council or the reverse?**

A. A member of the public cannot borrow local government funds. These are public funds and are intended for public utilities and services like health and education. A local government treasury therefore cannot be used as a loan fund.

However, a local government employee could be advanced a loan if rules and regulations allow for such advances or loans and provided repayment terms are strictly followed.

A local government can borrow in any way and from any source, as long as the conditions for borrowing are fulfilled and subject to the minister's approval, as required by law.

Q27.   Is it acceptable for a council to utilise 40% of its block grant funds in only one month?

A. A council operates on an approved budget. Budgets spread funds over twelve months of the financial year. It is not acceptable to spend 40% of the whole year's grant in one month.

The central government, however, anticipated such possibilities. Grants are released on a monthly basis, so that reckless local governments can be controlled through the "Release System". This system its has disadvantages, besides advantages like the one mentioned above. It can slow down the implementation of work plans.

Q28.   What is the rationale of having both a sub-accountant and a cashier at the sub-county level?

A. Under normal financial management practices, a system requires checks and balances. A sub-accountant is the person in charge of accounts. Duties of a sub-accountant are clearly described in the Financial and Accounting Regulations 1998 Regulation 178 of LGFAR. The cashier's responsibilities are also defined. A cashier accounts, to the sub-accountant for all the income received and money spent on a daily basis. The sub-accountant should cross-check this information and produce financial statements, which are eventually cross-checked by auditors, etc.

Section 5

Independent Bodies of Local Governments

Q1. **What should be done to ensure the independence of the District Service Commission?**

A. There is no specific solution to the problem of undermining the independence of a DSC. The most obvious solution would be to sensitise local government leadership about the independence of a body like DSC. Political leaders should understand the importance of checks and balances in good governance practices.

Secondly, it is necessary to involve representatives of the civic society organisations in the activities of DSC. These could sit on this commission as observers, to witness and expose any political interference.

Q2. **Can public officers be appointed to statutory bodies like DSC, or LGTB, etc.?**

A. Public officers do not qualify to be members of most of the statutory bodies.

Q3. **What are the qualifications required of a member of Public Service Commission?**

A. Qualifications are outlined in the Act, section 57 SS(a), the most important of which are:

(i) Have working experience of not less than 10 years.
(ii) Hold at least an Advanced Certificate of Education, plus a diploma.
(iii) Residence in high integrity and moral character.
(iv) Residence in the subject district.

Q4. **What has the government done to ensure that DSC do their work efficiently?**

A. (i) Since the Act came into force, members of the DSC have been paid from the Consolidated Fund. A district council therefore cannot not frustrate them. In case they are frustrated, they are entitled to report to higher authorities, for example, IGG.

(ii) The commissions are trained regularly, which has improved their efficiency and moral integrity.
(iii) From time to time, members of DSC have received various guidelines to help the commission make proper decisions.

Q5. **What powers does the Public Service Commission have over the District Service Commissions?**

A. Legally, the PSC does not have executive powers. For example, the PSC cannot nullify appointments made by the DSC. However, the PSC advises the DSCs and constitutionally co-ordinates the work.

Section 6

Institutions and Linkages

Q1. To whom is a chief administrative officer responsible?

A. A chief administrative officer is answerable to the district council. However, for day to day accountability, a CAO is answerable to the LC V chairperson, who is the political head of the district. A chief administrative officer is the head of the public service in a district, and the accounting officer.

Q2. What are the procedures for the removal of a Chief Administrative Officer or a Town Clerk?

A. The law provides that, before procedures to remove the CAO or the TC are initiated, at least following the grounds must exist:

(i) Abuse of office
(ii) Incompetence
(iii) Misconduct or misbehaviour
(iv) Physical or mental incapacity which renders the officer incapable of performing his/her duties.

Procedures for the removal of a CAO or TC

(i) Once any of the above causes have been established, a council, properly convened, passes a resolution supported by two thirds of the members, recommending the dismissal of the officer.

(ii) Before the council passes the resolution, the officer has a right to defend himself or herself, after receiving allegations in writing from the council.

(iii) Once the council has resolved to recommend the dismissal of the officer, the clerk to the council forwards its resolution, with supporting documents, to the chairperson of the District Service Commission.

(iv) The District Service Commission is then bound to interdict the officer but also to ask the officer concerned to submit his/her defence in writing, within fourteen days of receipt of the letter of interdiction.

(v) The DSC is also required to carry out investigations into the allegations against the officer. Investigations enable the DSC to take appropriate action.

(vi) Any fresh allegations or information found against the officer should be brought to his/her attention and the officer should be allowed to defend him/herself.

(vii) The decision of the DSC is not final. The officer is allowed to appeal to the Public Service Commission (PSC).

Q3. **When should the Minister of Local Government intervene to solve personnel wrangles in local governments?**

A. The model of decentralisation entrenched in the constitution leaves no room for direct intervention.

However, the minister could render advice where the law has not been followed. He/she could intervene indirectly by providing technical assistance where it is lacking and if it is believed to be a cause of the problem. Personnel wrangles, excluding political differences, should be resolved by the implications district leadership using the existing regulations, rules and, where necessary, the law.

Q4. **Does the chairperson of a sub-county or town council have any influence on the police deployed in his/her area of jurisdiction?**

A. A chairperson is the "highest" political leader in his/ her area of jurisdiction. Therefore the police should keep him/her informed. The influence should be positive, for example, the police relationship with the public. The chairperson should not interfere with the way police carries out its duties, which might be too technical for a non-professional to understand.

Since a chairperson is also responsible for the law and order in his/her area, he/she and the police have common interests in security matters.

Q5. **What protection do public servants have against pressure to implement unlawful decisions by councils?**

A. Public officers in a district are under the supervision of the Chief Administrative Officer (CAO). The CAO is also the adviser to the council on administrative and personnel matters.

The CAO is duty bound to advise the council against making illegal resolutions/decisions. If the council insists on passing an illegal decision, then the CAO should advise the executive committee that such a resolution cannot be implemented.

If the Executive Committee ignores the advice, the CAO can seek guidance from a relevant line ministry or the Ministry of Local Government.

However, some local governments have legal advisers. Councils are entitled to consult state Attorneys or other lawyers, especially where the legal advice of the Chief Administrative Officer is not trusted.

Q6.   **Are public servants at the sub-county paid salaries from the 65% of the revenue retained at that level?**

A. A sub-county does not employ established public officers. These are "seconded" officers by the district. The district pays them, mostly from their unconditional grants, which include a substantial element of salaries and wages.

A sub-county could have a few employees, most likely temporary employees for specific tasks that could be paid from own resources. These, if they exist, would not be on the district payroll.

Q7. If a public officer is dismissed for abuse of office, can he/she be compelled to pay losses he/she caused to the council?

A. Dismissal based on such grounds would be reached after investigations by organs of government, for example, Inspector General of Government or Auditor-General. Such bodies would make a recommendation(s) on such losses. If it is recommended that the officer pays back whatever losses he/she caused, then the council would have to implement the recommendations.

Q8. When will arrears of other categories of staff in local governments be paid, e.g. agricultural extension workers, teachers, etc.?

A. Arrears have been paid by the central government through the Ministry of Public Service. All categories of staff have been covered, except that some individuals in various categories may have been overlooked due to various reasons, for example verification problems.

Q9. Some districts have appealed to central government for assistance in paying retrenchment packages to those laid off as a result of restructuring. Is government likely to assist councils in paying the packages?

A. Restructuring policy originates from the central government and, generally, it is part of the overall reform programmes the government has carried out during the past ten years or more.

The central government, therefore, has the responsibility to pay retrenchment packages to those who are retrenched, under the government's policy.

If, however, a local government takes a decision outside the various reform programmes, then the centre is not obliged to pay the packages.

Q10. **There have been instances of diversion of delegated salaries to pay staff on the decentralised payroll and this has caused arrears. How will this problem be solved?**

A. Delegated staff: Delegated public officers are those who work in institutions or provide services that have not been decentralised to local government. Mostly, these include health workers in regional referral hospitals and secondary school teachers. Secondary schools, to date have not been decentralised.

Local governments, being nearer to where these officers work, have been entrusted with the responsibility of paying them, and funds are sent to the districts as conditional grants to pay salaries and wages of those categories of officers.

If a district diverts such funds, the central government has a number of options to take, including:

(i) Withholding unconditional grants and paying those whose salaries have been diverted.

(ii) Where applicable, withholding an equalisation grant to pay salaries of officers whose money has been diverted.

Q11.   **What are the functions of a sub-county chief, parish chief and sub-accountant?**

A. The following are the functions and responsibilities of each of those officers:

(i) Parish chief: A parish chief is the lowest employee of local government. He/she is in charge of a parish or a ward. He/she collects taxes, keeps tax-payer registers, registers of residents of the parish, and registers of shops and other assets that can bring revenue in the form of taxes. A parish chief also assists the LC I and LC II councils as their administrative officer. He/she budgets for these councils and acts as their accounting officer.

(ii) Sub-accountant is a title given to a technical officer in charge of keeping financial records and producing financial statements at the sub-county level. A sub-accountant should also assist institutions in the sub-county to write their books of accounts, especially primary schools and the health facilities, if such assistance is required.

A sub-accountant is answerable to the sub-county chief for all the revenue collected, the banking and transfers of funds to different levels of councils, for example, 35% to the district and other percentages to other councils. He/she should be in charge of graduated tax tickets, keep the safe keys and all records and financial transactions of a sub-county.

(iii) Sub-county chief is an accounting officer at the sub-county level. He/she is the most senior administrator and an advisor to LC III on administration, finance and personnel matters. He/she is responsible for co-ordination of staff of various sectors. He/she is answerable to the chairperson of LC III and to the Chief Administrative Officer at the district level.

Q12. **Which officer is responsible for the transfer of district council staff?**

A. The head of district service is the Chief Administrative Officer. He/she is responsible for the human resource management. However, he/she should work closely with the District Service Commission, if the intervention of the commission could be useful.

Q13. **What steps should be taken against chiefs who resist transfers?**

A. It is necessary to find out why the officer concerned is against the transfer and to explain why a transfer is necessary.

A transfer could be:

(i) In the interest of the employer and a disadvantage to the officer, in which case the officer should be persuaded to put the council's interest first.

(ii) In the interest of the officer if, for example, promotion is possible, in which case this possibility should also be explained.

(iii) Serve as punishment, in which case the officer should be handled by the District Service Commission and the reasons for the punishment should be explained.

Q14.   To whom is the sub-county chief responsible?

A. A sub-county chief is accountable to:

(i) The sub-county council (LC III) who is the "employer".

(ii) The chairperson of the executive committee at that level. The chairperson is the supervisor of the sub-county chief.

(iii) The Chief Administrative Officer who is the head of the district service. The CAO is also responsible for administrative supervision of the sub-county chief.

Q15.   If the person specifications of a post are raised by law, what happens to the incumbents who do not meet the qualifications?

A. If a post is upgraded, a number of options are available to the administration and the incumbents:

(i) If the incumbents have a sound basic education, it would be cheaper and more convenient to retrain such people and prepare them for more responsibilities, than dismissing them or retiring them. Training can be done on the job or formal training can be carried out.

(ii) Where retaining incumbents is not possible, it is appropriate to recruit new staff or transfer them from different departments to fill newly created positions.

Q16. Can the Ministry of Local Government organise quarterly seminars to review the implementation of decentralisation in Uganda?

A. Records indicate that the ministry has, on number of occasions, organised seminars on decentralisation in Uganda. This has been done annually, for example, from 1995 to 1999 annual national decentralisation review seminars were organised.

Q17. Is it possible for a public servant to transfer from one district to another without it affecting his/her service?

A. Each district service is independent of the other. However, the national service is one, i.e. the terms of service are common throughout the service.

In order to transfer, agreement is necessary between the district from where the officer wants to move and the district to which the officer wants to go. The District Service Commission to which the officer wishes to go should accept to recruit that officer in that district service.

Q18. What is the maximum period a public servant should take at a station?

A. Standing orders do not state how long an officer should stay at one particular station. The decentralisation of the civil service has advantages and disadvantages. Before decentralisation, a public officer could work anywhere in Uganda. There was flexibility in terms of transfers from one district to another.

Since the service has been decentralised, it is likely that an officer would work in one district until he/she retires or transfers, either to the centre or to another district. However, where applicable, transfers within the district are possible.

Q19.   If a new district is created out of an existing district by parliament, are public officers who are taken over by the new district reinterviewed and reappointed?

A. If officers had been appointed by a competent authority (District Service Commission) there would be no need to reinterview them. This would be the normal position. However, should a district (a new one) not require all existing employees, and decides to select on interview basis, such a procedure would be acceptable.

Q20.   Can a sub-county council recommend the transfer of a public servant who is a non-performer?

A. All employees in a district are employees of the district. A sub-county may not ask for a transfer as such but can ask the head of the district service to recall an officer. The CAO decides whether to transfer such an officer to another sub-county or deploy him/her at the headquarters.

A sub-county chief, as head of service at that level, should also make firm recommendations about an officer. If the officer is a non-performer, the sub-county should find out why, e.g. age, poor educational background or lack of interest An officer needs help e.g. retraining or motivation.

Q21. **Who supervises the local defence force unit at sub-county level?**

A. Local defence force units form part of security establishments. Under normal circumstances they should be supervised by security personnel, either from the police or army. There should be co-ordination with the sub-county administration, particularly the chairperson and the sub-county chief. All the police personnel have been transferred to the Ministry of Internal Affairs. It is this ministry which supervises the local police.

Q22. **Can a Chief Administrative Officer discipline a public servant on the advice of a district chairperson without the entire council's involvement?**

A. A chairperson of a district executive committee may not "advise" the Chief Administrative Officer. The CAO is supposed to discipline public officers long before the intervention of political leaders, and get to know the behaviours of such officers.

Should it happen that the chairperson obtains details about the behaviour of a public officer before the CAO takes action or before he/she is informed about the behaviour of the officer, then the chairperson would bring to the attention of the CAO the behaviour of such an officer. He/she should not propose the disciplinary action to be taken. That remains a responsibility of the DSC and the CAO.

Q23. **If a District Service Commission directs the removal of a public officer, does he or she receive terminal benefits?**

A. A District Service Commission is normally guided by the standing orders, circulars, etc. regarding management of the public service.

i) In most cases, a decision of the DSC on how a public officer is to be disciplined, depends on a number of factors, for example, whether the disciplinary action is being taken for the first time.

(ii) The nature of the decision is also influenced by the gravity of the crime committed by the officer, for example, if the officer has been involved in serious corruption, he/she could be dismissed without any retirement benefits.

(iii) The extent to which the officer is directly involved in the "crime", for example, an accounting officer could have over-trusted his/her subordinate staff to the extent that small amounts of money have been stolen. In such cases, a DSC could recommend retirement of the officer with full benefits.

There are three possible levels of action a District Service Commission could take:

(i)   Retirement in public interest
(ii) Dismissal for gross misbehaviour
(iii) Termination of services of the officer by the council outside the agreed or civil service terms of service.

Q24. **If an officer goes up-country on a weekend in his/her official vehicle, who should pay the driver's allowances in such circumstances?**

A. In the first place, an officer should not travel in an official car to visit his/her up-country home, unless he/she is entitled to such facilities and it is clearly stated in his/her letter of appointment. Without such entitlement, it is assumed that the vehicle is to be used for official travel only, and from home to office and back. In case of any illegal journey, the government would not be held responsible for any kind of payment to a third party.

Q25. **Why do local governments pay salaries late?**

A. Some local governments pay salaries late because:

(i)   Districts receive unconditional grants late, from which the salaries of most of the public officers are paid.
(ii) Sometimes, employees receive their salaries late from the local revenue collections due to local governments' cash flow problems resulting from poor local revenue collections.
(iii) Late salary payments may result from poor financial management. In such cases, councils

fail to adjust the budgets according to available resources, or even spend money on activities that do not appear in the estimates.

(iv) The council may fail to meet its prompt salary payment obligations owing to the incompetence of employees. Staff in the financial department may fail to process payment on time, even when funds are available.

Q26.   What happens if temporary appointment of a public officer exceeds 12 months?

A. Since temporary appointments are no longer by practice the government, it is not possible to answer the question. However, should a local government take on anybody on temporary terms, his/her terms of employment should be clearly spelt out and accepted by the employee.

Q27.   Has the function of recruiting and appointing secondary school teachers been decentralised?

A. Under the second schedule of the local governments Act 1997, secondary schools are supposed to have been decentralised. However, in practice this has not happened as yet, and the appointment, disciplinary actions, promotions, etc. are still being done by the Teaching Service Commission at headquarters. This anomaly can be attributed to the provision in the constitution that decentralisation would be implemented in a co-ordinated manner. In that case, it is assumed that modalities to transfer the responsibilities to local governments have not been completed.

Q28. **Why should delegated staff fill the same performance appraisal forms when they are not staff of ministries?**

A. The purpose of appraisal forms is to help management assess the performance of staff. Whether the staff is delegated or an employee of the local government does not make much difference. The objective is the same.

Government is nowadays concerned about achievement or results oriented management. The forms should be suitable for both local employees and delegated staff if a result-oriented approach is used to assess the performance of any of those categories.

Q29. **If a District Service Commission directs the promotion of a public officer, who should pay for the increments due to the officer?**

A. A District Service Commission serves local governments in a district. This refers to both the district and the urban council staff. Therefore the staff who are affected by the decision of the DSC falls into those two categories i.e. either the district is responsible for the decision of the DSC or the urban councils are.

Q30. **When should an officer be interdicted and/or removed from office?**

A. Interdiction or dismissal etc. are the responsibility of a District Service Commission. Standing orders and other instruments give guidance, but the actual decision remains with the DSC. It bases its judgement on evidence given by the accuser. The Chief Administrative Officer would normally submit a request for interdiction or dismissal if there is enough grounds for such a serious decision. The commission would normally give the officer an opportunity to respond to the accusations from the CAO. The officer can also appeal against the DSC if they decide to either interdict or dismiss him/her. The appeal is referred to the Public Service Commission. Cases are also known where public officers have approached courts of law.

Q31.   What arrangements exist for payment of pensions and gratuities?

A. The former central government staff are treated like any other public officer who decides to retire or who is retrenched. Such officers therefore follow normal procedures of retirement or retrenchment, etc.

Q32.   What are the views of the minister about public officers who remain interdicted for more than a year? Should they return to work without further delay?

A. Where an officer has been unfairly treated by keeping him/her on interdiction for unnecessarily long, he/she could appeal to higher authorities. For example, he/she could appeal to the Public Service Commission or the Inspector General of Government, or even to the minister responsible for local governments.

Q33. **How does a Resident District Commissioner get information he/she may require from the local government?**

A. A Resident District Commissioner's responsibilities are outlined in section 72 of the Local Governments Act No 1 of 1997. Among those duties, the law requires him/her to monitor and inspect activities of local governments. The RDC, therefore, can obtain information directly from the source, for example, he/she can visit health facilities, schools or any other institution and obtain information from the public officers who serve in these institutions.

Secondly, the RDC can obtain information from the local council i.e. the chairperson of a district, municipal council or sub-county council.

The RDC is also empowered to ask the chairperson to instruct the chief internal auditor to carry out a special audit. After such an audit, it is reasonably assumed that the RDC would demand a copy of the report.

The RDC also can ask the Auditor General to carry out a special investigation. He/she can do the same with the IGG. These bodies would give a copy of their report to the RDC.

Q34. **How often should local governments review their organisation structures?**

A. Unfortunately, the review of local government structures is not a responsibility of local governments themselves. The mandate to do such a review is a privilege of the central government. Structures of local governments affect the rest of the government. It is therefore understandable that those structures are reviewed by the centre to ensure that uniformity exists and any financial implications are assessed, costed and included in the grant structure.

Q35.   When will the decentralisation of the payroll to the districts be effected?

A. Decentralisation has so far seen a number of services and functions transferred from the centre to local governments. However, the payroll has remained a central function. The main reasons given include the fact that:

(i)   Not all functions have so far been transferred, for example, secondary schools have not yet been transferred to local government.

(ii)   Local governments do not have the capacity to run payrolls.

(iii) At this stage central government wishes to retain powers to control numbers in the whole civil service, as part of macro-economic management policy.

Given that the centre has interests in the district payrolls, it is not clear how long it will take to allow each district to prepare its own payroll. Local governments have to assure the government that they (local governments) are able to exercise discipline in the recruitment of staff, etc. In the meantime, partial decentralisation is being done through specific functions, for example batching.

Q36. Can a teacher, teaching in more than one government secondary school, be on the payroll of each of those schools where he/she teaches?

A. A teacher can only be on a payroll of the school which employees him/her as a full-time teacher. Elsewhere he/she teaches as a part-time teacher and most likely he/she is paid out of funds contributed by parents. It would be illegal therefore for a teacher to be on more than one pay roll.

Q37. Why can't the chief administrative officer be appointed on contract terms, like permanent secretaries?

A. There is nothing to prevent District Service Commissions from appointing a CAO on contract terms. It all depends on the wishes of the district, age of the applicant and his/her working experience and background. If a selected applicant has been in the civil service and it benefits him/her to continue serving as a permanent and pensionable officer, such an officer is likely to negotiate similar terms to continue.

Q38. Why are a number of teachers not on the payroll?

A. There are several reasons why all teachers are not on the payroll.

  (i) There are many responsible officers involved in the teachers' payroll, for example the school where the teacher is posted, a district education officer, the CAO as accounting officer, the

Ministry of Education, the Teaching Service Commission and the Ministry of Public Service. It is quite possible to make a mistake at any one of those responsibility centres.

(ii) Allegations have also been made of corruption or abuse of office where, for instance, a headmaster deliberately omits a teacher because of some disagreement.

(iii) Thirdly, there are problems of documentation. These include original documents like certificates, appointment letters, registration of a teacher after confirmation, etc.

Q39.   Who keeps the confidential files for the town clerk and the Chief Administrative Officer?

A. These could keep more than one confidential file:

(i) The chairperson of a district, for instance, could keep a confidential file of the CAO. Also, a District Service Commission, particularly the chairperson, should have a confidential file of the CAO.

(ii) A file of a Town Clerk may similarly be kept by his/her chairperson and, particularly by the CAO as the head of the district service and the DSC chairperson.

Q40.   When allocating scholarships, should the government also consider awarding them to staff of local governments so that they improve on their skills?

A. Training has generally remained a responsibility of the centre. The line ministries, therefore, are responsible for drawing up training programmes that should involve local government staff. This has already been done by some ministries, for example Ministry of Health.

Local governments also receive direct assistance from donors for training, for example DANIDA has trained many local government staff over years. Rakai District has, perhaps, benefited more than any other district.

Q41. Some districts operate two payrolls. Why are the payrolls not integrated into one?

A. Payrolls are actually integrated, and both previous employees of the centre and locally recruited staff are on one payroll identified by different codes, for example, "L" for locally recruited staff. However, some districts have not "owned" the payroll on which former central employees appear. There is, therefore, a need to sensitise such local governments.

Q42. Are public officers protected from arbitrary removal from office?

A. Public officers are protected from arbitrary decisions in many ways. However, the most important protection is for the political leaders and administrators to understand rules and regulations that govern civil servants. The civil servants themselves should refrain from political activities which could cause them problems.

A body which protects district civil servants is the District Service Commission. Political leaders should not arbitrarily dismiss public officers without the intervention of DSC. The procedures alone indicate the level of protection. The following prerequisites have to be fulfilled:

(i)   A public officer has a right to defend him/herself against any accusations against him/her.

(ii)   Not every accusation results into dismissal. In some cases, it could lead to a warning or at worst a suspension.

(iii) Where an unfair decision is taken against the officer, the officer has a right to appeal to various organs at the centre. These include IGG, etc. If the officer is still dissatisfied with decisions of administrative organs, he/she could take the council to courts of law. Many local authorities, particularly district councils, have paid heavy compensation as a result of court intervention.

Section 7

Personal Payments

Q1. **What are the entitled allowances for sub-county councillors?**

A. Payments to councillors are regulated under the first schedule of the Act. In general, the following officers are entitled to payments:

(i)   Chairpersons of local governments
(ii) Vice-chairpersons
(iii) The third category comprises the secretaries at District Council level (full time) and the vice-chairpersons of municipal councils.

Councillors at sub-county level are normally entitled to allowances for:

(i)   Travelling (transport)
(ii) Subsistence
(iii) Sitting
(iv) Safari day

A sub-county council normally decides the amount payable to councillors, but the total expenditure in any one year should not exceed 20% of the total income (actual) generated by the council.

Q2. **Are signatories to local government bank accounts entitled to allowances?**

A. Signatories should not be paid any allowances. In most cases, such signatories are public officers and sign documents as part of their duties. Even in rare cases where the council decides to have an outsider to sign financial documents, such a person would not be entitled to any payment.

Q3.   What is the current policy on emoluments for statutory board members?

A. With exception of the District Land Board, members of all other statutory boards i.e., the District Service Commission, the Local Governments Tender Board, and Local Governments Public Accounts Committee members are paid by the central government. Payments are based on prevailing central government rules and regulations.

Q4.   Who is responsible for payment of allowances to technical staff deployed at sub-county, city or municipal division levels?

A. Public officers in a district are employees of that district regardless of the deployment of such officers. The same applies to the municipal council. All employees belong to the municipal council, though they might work for a division.

Payment of salaries and wages is not devolved to lower level local governments. The same should apply to allowances. However, a sub-county or division could, within its mandates, make payment of some allowances where the claim could arise from activities initiated by that council, for example, where the council has a special project which requires the officer to spend outside his/her station.

Q5. Can executive committee members of a sub-county, city or municipal division, receive allowances when they attend council meetings?

A. The first schedule of the Act gives details of allowances to be paid. As long as members of any executive committee do not receive monthly salaries and are not appointed full time, they would be entitled to allowances whenever they attend council meetings. They would also be paid if called to attend executive committee meetings (lower local governments).

Q6. Why do lunch allowances of district health staff differ from those of the hospital?

A. The allowances do not differ as such. However, clarification is necessary:

(i) Established staff, regardless of where they are employed, are being paid Shs. 66 000 per month. On the other hand, support staff, mostly those without formal professional qualifications, are being paid Shs. 44 000 per month.

(ii) It is also possible that some districts did not pay full amount of allowances as expected. This could cause a difference and complaints based on such irregularities being received by the central ministry responsible for health service delivery.

Q7. Why doesn't central government cater for the emoluments of the local councillors?

A. There are a number of reasons why the centre left this responsibility to the local councils themselves:

(i)   Payments to councillors should be handled by those who are involved with them on a daily basis and who know why they are paid (services rendered). The centre does not know how much night allowance should be paid in relation to meeting(s) attended.

(ii)   Secondly, the constitution and the Act have empowered local governments to collect taxes and other revenues. It was considered appropriate that, among other items of expenditure, payments to councillors should be included. Since councils can regulate activities of councillors, it would be possible to control this expenditure in the same way.

(iii) Thirdly, councillors' allowances are based on the actual revenue being collected. Councillors should take an interest in the collection of local revenue as it affects their earnings. If they paid from the centre, they are (councillors) are likely to ignore the importance of local revenue collection.

Q8.   From where do councillors receive allowances for monitoring?

A. A councillor represents a specific constituency where he/she resides. It is assumed that a councillor can monitor activities within the constituency without extra cost. However, should a council feel that councillors require extra funding in order to carry out monitoring, then that council should budget for such expenditure.

Some programmes, for example those under PAF, have funds available for monitoring. In case a line ministry is in agreement that councillors should carry out monitoring, such funds can be used. The Ministry of Health, for instance, involves councillors in quality of service monitoring. Councillors form part of teams which visit health facilities. In that case, they are paid from PAF funds.

Q9. Do councillors qualify for payments or advances?

A. Allowances to councillors are paid under the first schedule of the Act. This schedule provides guidelines regarding how and how much councillors should be paid. It does not, however, provide for advance payment. As a rule, allowances are paid for a specific purpose, for example, transportation to enable a councillor attend meetings. Allowances, therefore, are not salaries. Allowances are paid to public officers and, where it is possible, paid in advance.

Q10. What would happen to a person who draws a salary as a civil servant while he/she is a councillor in the same council?

A. Currently, the law does not allow a civil servant to be a councillor and remain on the payroll of the district or any other lower local government. Once a civil servant is elected as a councillor, then he/she should resign the public office.

Q11.   **Why don't district councillors who resign their civil service positions receive monthly emoluments, in keeping with economic realities, as district councils may take long to sit?**

A. Such arrangements do not exist. Once someone decides to be a councillor, then he/she should accept the terms attached to that position. It would not be possible to treat former civil servants differently from other councillors who live within the same environment.

Q12.   **Does the 20% regulation refer only to locally generated funds, or the conditional grants as well?**

A. The percentage in the regulations of the first schedule refers to the locally raised revenue. The implications are that the more a local government collects, the more it can pay its councillors (in terms of reasonable amount for specific purposes as indicated in the regulations).

Q13.   **Should a councillor's allowances be taxed and by what percentage?**

A. Uganda Revenue Authority is in charge of taxation. They advise all employers and their institutions who should be taxed and by how much. Local government councils are, therefore, subject to guidelines which may change from one financial year to another. If the law requires that certain allowances should be taxed, then the finance department has an obligation to deduct the appropriate amount from the councillors' allowances.

Q14. **Is it proper for the sub-county chairperson to draw a consolidated allowance, which is not allowed for other councillors?**

A. A sub-county council can consolidate allowances of its chairperson, provided no other allowances are paid in addition to the consolidated allowance. Other councillors may not receive consolidated allowances because of different responsibilities. A chairperson carries more responsibilities than any other councillor.

Q15. **Why do only medical staff receive lunch allowances?**

A. There are genuine reasons for this "positive discrimination" in the payment of lunch allowances.

(i) Medical staff work longer hours than other officers. In most cases, they work during their lunch hour. Allowances, therefore, compensate for the missed lunch and time spent on duty saving lives.

(ii) The line ministry (Ministry of Health) took the initiative to negotiate for this special allowance, that has since been consolidated into the salary structure of health workers.

Q16.   Why is there a disparity in the salary structure of medical staff and other civil servants at the same level/salary scale?

A. Medical staff are classified as essential service workers. They work during holidays, at night, and longer hours than other public workers. They are normally on call i.e. they can be called upon at any time in the case of emergency.

Secondly, many medical workers can be persuaded to leave the service and replacing them is difficult. Most professionals in the medical field take years to train and some specialised training is not even available in this country.

Q17.   Is it in order for head teachers and teachers' representatives on the Board of Governors to receive sitting allowances?

A. Any institution or organisation is controlled by rules and regulations. In the case of Boards of Governors of schools, the Ministry of Education and Sports has put in place rules and regulations which spell out entitlements for those who sit on those boards. If the rules, therefore, authorise payment to that category of members, then it would be in order.

Secondly, such payment serves as a recognition of the contribution that individual members make towards the management of the institution. Furthermore, people spend time attending meetings, for example, a headmaster has a number of activities he has to attend to in a day. When time is lost in meetings, sacrifices have to be made to compensate. Payment of that nature, therefore, motivates a person who has made a sacrifice.

Q18. **Are pensioners entitled to annual increments when the government increases wages and salaries?**

A. Pensions are not increased annually as salaries are. However, government has revised pensions payable to retired civil servants. This seems to have been a special consideration due to the low amount which was being paid.

Q19. **If a public servant and / or members of a statutory body are dismissed, but they are on appeal within the courts of law, who should pay for such expenditure for which budget has been allocated?**

A. Councils are normally advised not to rush into decisions. Once proper procedures have been followed, such a situation would rarely arise. In the first place, officers should be interdicted on half their salaries until all investigations and appeals have been completed.

However, if procedures are ignored, the council would normally meet the costs. The total costs would include:

(i)   One year's salary
(ii) Pension

(iii) Basic salary in lieu of earned leave, etc.
(iv) Severance package
(v)   Transport expenses, etc.

Q20.   Do benefits such as water, shamba-boy and electricity, to which district chairpersons are entitled, form a part of the 15% of the total local revenue collected by the local government council in the previous financial year?

A. The current regulations indicate that such expenses form part of the total amount payable to the chairperson and does not, therefore, form part of the 20% of the actual revenue collected during the previous financial year.

Q21.   Do ex-officials merit any allowances if they attend meetings?

A. Ex-officials do not receive any allowances when they attend council or other meetings intended for elected officials. They attend such meetings to give explanations when required to do so, mainly by political leaders. They should be considered to be on duty.

Q22.   What happens if the 20% a council is supposed to spend on council expenses cannot sustain the council's programmes in a given year?

A. A local government has a system enabling it to operate under different situations. Part of the system is budgeting. A local government has to operate a budget and that budget should take into consideration the available resources. A council must, at any rate, be able to collect revenue. Whatever is collected, 20% of it must be set aside for councillors' allowances, etc. This amount could be much less than the previous two years or less than what neighbouring councils are paying. However, it should be considered "enough" for the purpose for which it is intended and the budget for councillors should be made to "fit in".

Q23. **How can a sub-county council collect revenue without increasing its personnel, which has financial implications?**

A. It is true that at sub-county level, human resources is limited. Basically, there are three public officers, namely, the sub-county chief, the sub-accountant and the cashier. However, that team is supposed to be supported by the parish chiefs. Even then it could be difficult to mobilise local revenue with so few employees.

The solution lies in the privatisation of the collection of some revenue sources – market dues, licences, etc. should be privatised so that officials "chase" only a few collectors.

Q24. **If a financial year ends without a councillor receiving his/her salary, can he/she claim for arrears in the subsequent financial year?**

A. A councillor does not earn a salary, but allowances. These are specified in the first schedule of the Act. The councillor is paid allowances for:

(i)   Attending meetings

(ii) Overnight stays away from home while on official duty.

(iii) Travelling from home and back.

It would be in order to work out what the councillor "earned" during the previous financial year and pay him/her arrear, of allowances, not salary.

Q25.   Are motivation allowances acceptable for heads of departments and sub-county chiefs?

A. A council may pay motivation allowances, or any other allowances to its employees if such allowances are legal and properly authorised.

In all cases of payments, the most important point is the procedure and authority:

(i)   Expenditure must have been budgeted for in the local council's budget.

(ii) Authority to pay must be sought from relevant officials.

(iii) The relevant authorities should approve individuals to receive such allowances.

(iv) Purpose and origin of the payment must be clearly stated so that auditors do not raise queries.

Q26.   If an executive member of a district council resigns, does he/she merit any take-home package?

A. The terms of service of councillors, members of the executive committee, etc. are found in the first schedule of the Act. There are no suggested retirement benefits or packages of any type in such a situation. It is not, therefore, possible to pay any package to any member of the executive committee who resigns.

Q27. **Is it feasible for an internal auditor who is on his/her routine job to receive allowances whenever he/she visits the sub-county level?**

A. It is extremely dangerous for an auditor to draw any type of allowances from the station where he/she works. Auditors should carry sufficient allowances from the employer, i.e. the district. Any advances of allowances could compromise them in the execution of their duties.

Section 8

Procurement

Q1. **Can councillors be awarded tenders in the local governments they represent?**

A. The government has put in place Financial and Accounting Regulations for local government officials to follow. These were issued in May 1998 and they prohibit officials from tendering for services, goods and works in the councils where they are either employees or councillors. A councillor, therefore, may not be awarded any tender in the council she/he serves.

Q2. **What is the procurement process at sub-county, city or municipal division? What about at the district and municipal level?**

A. (i) Procurement procedures at sub-county level.
The law does not establish a separate Local Government Tender Board for a sub-county (LC III) local government. A sub-county, therefore, uses the District Local Government Tender Board.
The technical staff at the district level and those at the sub-county level assist with documentation, preparation of bid documents, etc. The requirements should be given to the secretary of the Local Government Tender Board to prepare

one procurement plan for the whole district and reduce costs of advertisements.

(ii) Procurement procedures at municipal level. A division council of a municipal or city council is legally entitled to establish its own Tender Board and follow procedures that are followed by the Municipal or City Council Tender Board and apply regulations in the Local Governments Financial and Accounting Regulations 1998, and any other regulations that might be issued.

(iii) Once a Tender Board has been established legally, regardless of level of local government, the procedures to be followed are the same, except that the membership of its Urban Tender Boards companies only five members, compared to seven for the District Local Government Tender Board.

Q3.   If tenders are awarded without going through the District or Urban Tender Board, what can the council do?

A. The tendering process is intended to ensure a transparent process. If not followed, those in authority have an obligation to act and rectify the situation.

(i) If a head of department awards tenders without authority of the Tender Board, the accounting officer, i.e. the CAO or the Town Clerk, has an obligation to cancel such an illegal award.

(ii) If the accounting officer is directly involved, the Local Governments Financial and Accounting Regulations empower the minister to intervene and nullify such tenders. It is also possible for the IGG to intervene in such cases.

However, a council also has a right to intervene the Executive Committee on behalf of the council if proper procedures had not been followed by the administrators. The chairperson of the Executive Committee can ask the CAO or Town Clerk to provide an explanation for irregularities. The chairperson of the district can ask the minister to nullify any tenders awarded through irregular procedure.

Q4.   Why don't sub-counties, city or municipal divisions appoint their own tender boards?

A. The law does not allow a sub-county to have its own Tender Board. Though reasons are not given, it may include the following:

(i)   Too expensive for a sub-county to have its own Tender Board.

(ii)   Lack of manpower at sub-county level to man a Tender Board.

(iii) Volume of business to be done by a Tender Board at that level not sufficient to justify establishment of a separate Tender Board.

On the other hand, an urban authority is allowed to appoint its own Tender Board. This means that the municipal and city divisions are free to appoint their own Tender Boards. However, the expenses of such Tender Boards are met by the councils themselves and not by the central government, from the consolidated fund, is as the case with the District Tender Boards.

Q5. The guide on procurement outside the Tender Board system stipulates that the limit for heads of departments is Shs. 1 000 000 for works and 500 000 for goods. Does this amount refer to a single purchase or total purchases throughout the F/Y?

A. The above amounts refer to single purchases or award in case of works. These awards or purchases refer to expenditure during the period when the LGTB is not transacting business and when it would be too expensive to call the Board to consider such an award. However, after purchases have been done, a report should be made to the LGTB with full facts, including background to the purchases of such goods or award of contract. In most cases, such purchases or awards are done in emergencies, for example, a bridge has been washed away during heavy rains and communication has been disrupted with or urgent stationery or other supplies, such as purchase of motor-vehicle tyres, that were not anticipated.

Under normal circumstances, such awards for purchases should be given to suppliers or contractors already approved by the LGTB, a minimum of three should be selected for quotation and the cheapest taken, unless there are reasons why the cheapest should not be awarded the contract.

Q6.   What is the provision on a councillor(s) contracting using a company or names that belong to him/her?

A. Councillors and employees of local governments are not allowed to supply or provide services under the tendering arrangement, mainly to avoid conflict of interest. During the process, the same officials may make decisions that conflict with their own interests whether or not they use false names or create companies. The way out, therefore, is not to supply under any name.

Q7.   What is the role of the works committees in awarding tenders for petty contracts?

A. A works committee should play a useful role in awarding petty contracts.   However, it should be guided by the technical staff of the works department. The committees should ensure transparency and value for money during the process of recommending such awards. Their job would be to recommend. In such a situation the committee would work closely with the technical evaluation committee.

Q8.   What system is in place for monitoring the performance of tenders?

A. There are three types of tenderers or suppliers of goods and services.

(i)   Suppliers of goods: There must be an agreed time-table for delivery of goods, and quantities and the quality to be delivered must be specified, before payment is made. Under normal circumstances, payment cannot be made before goods are supplied and quality and quantities ascertained.

(ii) Suppliers of works: Detailed procedures should be in place. This would be indicated in the contract, for example, visits to the sites and site meetings to be held and review of the performance of the contractor. In addition, however, heads of departments involved should make regular progress reports to the relevant committee of the council and the accounting officer.

(iii) Service contracts: These are mainly consultancies. In some cases, local governments may lack the expertise to supervise complicated service contracts or consultancies. In such cases, it would be in order to employ other consultants to assist a local government in supervising another service provider.

Q9. **What is the role of the secretary to the Local Government Tender Board?**

A. The law requires a Tender Board to have a secretary whose main duties include the following:

(i) In consultation with the chairperson, convening meetings of the Tender Board.

(ii) In consultation with the accounting officer and heads of department, compiling tender requirements to be advertised in national newspapers (and on notice boards).

(iii) Keeping all records of proceedings of the Tender Board business (minutes).

(iv) Distributing minutes to all authorised recipients, including the ministry and IGG.

(v) Notifying heads of department of awards made.

(vi) Co-ordinating sub-county tendering needs and ensuring that their requirements are compiled and included in the work plans of the LGTB.

(vii) Organising contracts to be entered into between local governments and the suppliers.

Q10.   Can a district chairperson remove a member of a statutory body, for example, LGTB?

A. The chairperson may not act alone. He/she acts on behalf of the Executive Committee. A procedure is to be followed to remove any member of a statutory body. Also, there must be reasons for removing such a person. The following reasons are valid:

(i)   Abuse of office

(ii) Incompetence

(iii) Failure to attend meetings without good reasons acceptable to the Board

(iv) Failure to declare pecuniary interest

Q11.   Is it in order for technocrats other than the secretary to attend Tender Board Meetings?

A. (i)   The law requires the secretary to be in attendance throughout the business of the Tender Board. A situation could arise where a head of department whose procurement needs are being discussed is invited to brief the Board. It is assumed that, after giving the necessary brief, the Board would ask him/her to leave the meeting.

(ii) The Board could also invite the Technical Evaluation Committee members (technocrats) to attend a meeting of the Board and brief it on their recommendations. However, it is advisable that, when the Board is fully briefed and before the actual award takes place, public officers leave the Board meeting to enable the Board to take independent decisions.

Q12. **Under what circumstances can the contract between a tenderer and the council be terminated?**

A. Most contracts allow for, termination of contracts. Either party can give notice, or specific conditions can lead to termination of contracts, for example, social and economic conditions. However, the client can terminate a contract if the work is not satisfactory and the contractor has failed to improve after being warned, in accordance with the terms of the contract.

Q13. **Can town councils appoint their own Tender Boards?**

A. The Local Governments Act prescribes that an urban authority either uses a District Local Government Tender Board (LGTB) or opt for its own Tender Board. However, there is a cost involved if an urban authority decides to have its own Tender Board.

(i) It would have to recall its representative from the District Local Government Tender Board.

(ii)   It would have to meet all the costs involved in running that Urban Tender Board. The District Local Government Tender Board is normally financed by the central government, from the consolidated fund. This same financial assistance is not available to an Urban Tender Board.

Q14.   Can the district local governments tender boards give preferential treatment to youth associates and groups in bidding for rural markets, landing sites, and rural roads tolls management?

A.   There is no provision in the law and other regulations to support youth associations in the tendering process. If it were possible, it would introduce an anomaly in the process and the system could be abused.

The objective of tendering is to achieve the best and efficient supplier or contractor. Through such efficiency, local governments would benefit and such benefits would reach other institutions that depend on the local government system.

Q15.   What action can the Inspector-General of Government (IGG), the minister responsible for local governments, and the district council take against a corrupt Local Government Tender Board?

A.   Before action can be taken there is a need to establish that corruption actually exists. Once this has been done, a number of options exist:

(i) The minister can ask the council to take action against the LGTB. The minister does not have direct powers to dismiss the Board. In such a situation, reasons are available under the law, for example, abuse of office can apply.

(ii) The IGG can investigate under its own powers and direct the dismissal of the Tender Board members once it has been established that corruption exists.

Q16. Which officer is responsible for making purchases at the sub-county level?

A. Generally, all purchases, whether at sub-county or district level, are made in the name of the Accounting Officer. At the sub-county level, a sub-county chief is the Accounting Officer. He/she must authorise purchases, whether through the proper tendering process or any other approach.

Q17. Why doesn't the right to tender markets in sub-county revert to lower councils other than the district Local Government Tender Board?

A. The District Local government Tender Board must work for all councils in a district. The lower local governments and administrative units do not have the capacity to run Local Government Tender Boards of their own. In the case of rural markets, therefore, the issue is who does the documentation and requests the tender to act? Another issue to consider is who collects revenue from those markets? Revenue collection is the most important. If a sub-county collects the revenue and distributes it according to the law, then it would not really matter much who instructed the tender board to tender out the revenue collection in first place.

Q18.   Is the requirement that anything above Shs. 500 000 must be subjected to the tendering process a waste of time and a disrespect for decentralisation?

A. The requirement that any supply valued at more than Shs. 500 000 must go through the tendering process, as must works exceeding Shs. 1 000 000 in value, is a safeguard for decentralisation. Transparency and accountability are extremely important if decentralisation is to survive and prosper.

Procurement is one way in which corruption could penetrate the system, to the disadvantage of taxpayers.

Index